D1442122

118785286

A Tribute to
THE YOUNG AT HEART

BILL PEET

By Jill C. Wheeler

Published by Abdo & Daughters, 4940 Viking Drive, Suite 622, Edina, Minnesota 55435.

Library bound edition distributed by Rockbottom Books, Pentagon Tower, P.O. Box 36036, Minneapolis, Minnesota 55435.

Cover Photo credit: Gale Research
Interior Photo credits: Bettmann Archives, pages 11, 20
Wide World Photos, pages 15, 21, 23
Gale Research, page 29

Edited by Julie Berg

LIBRARY OF CONGRESS CATALOGING-IN-PUBLICATION DATA

Wheeler, Jill C., 1964-
     Bill Peet / Jill C. Wheeler.
     p.   cm. -- (The young at heart)
Includes index.
Summary: Biography of the American author, illustrator, and animator whose drawings include many details and whose characters are often warm and friendly.
     ISBN 1-56239-491-6
1. Peet, Bill--Biography--Juvenile literature. 2. Authors, American--20th century--Biography--Juvenile literature. 3. Children's stories--Authorship--Juvenile literature. 4. Illustrators--United States--Biography--Juvenile literature. 5. Animators--United States--Biography--Juvenile literature. 6. Walt Disney Productions--Juvenile literature. [1. Peet, Bill. 2. Authors, American. 3. Illustrators.] I. Title. II . Series: Tribute to the young at heart.
PS3566.E29Z94 1996
741.6'42'092--dc20
[B]   95-41216
                                                                              CIP
                                                                               AC

Table of Contents

WHY, IT'S A WHINGDINGDILLY!

Children's book author, Bill Peet, loves to spend time with children. He often travels to elementary schools to talk and draw with students. He enjoys playing a special game with them. He stands at the blackboard and begins to draw an animal. The children have to guess what animal he is drawing.

Usually, the students guess correctly before he finishes drawing. On one school visit, Peet tried something different. He started drawing one animal until the students guessed what it was. Peet said, "No," and drew part of a different animal on the same drawing.

When he finished, the drawing had parts of a giraffe, an elephant, a camel, a zebra, a reindeer, a rhino and a dog. No one could guess what it was. Peet made up a name. He called it a "whingdingdilly." The drawing inspired him to write a book by that name. It's about a dog that wants to be different and finds a witch to help him.

Peet has been drawing for as long as he can remember. His work has touched the lives of millions of young people. He has written and illustrated more than 30 children's books. Publishers have translated his books into other languages. He wrote and illustrated two famous Walt Disney movies — *One Hundred and One Dalmatians* and *The Sword in the Stone*.

Peet's drawings range from silly to ridiculous. Yet whatever he draws, he draws it well. That's because he loves it.

"Drawing became my number one hobby as soon as I could manipulate a crayon or pencil well enough to put my favorite things on paper," he said. Even the Depression couldn't stop him from his love of art. "For me the best of all nickel bargains was a box of crayons."

HOOSIER BEGINNINGS

Peet was born on January 19, 1915, near Indianapolis, Indiana. Peet calls himself a Hoosier. A Hoosier is a nickname for someone from Indiana.

Peet had an unusual childhood. When he was only three years old, his father, Orion, was drafted into the military. World War I ended before Orion had to go to Europe to fight. Yet Orion never returned to his family. He became a traveling salesman instead.

Peet, his mother, and his brothers moved to Indianapolis, Indiana, to live with Peet's grandmother. Peet loved it because her house was close to the country where he could play. Yet his favorite activity could take place anywhere.

"My favorite room in the house was the attic, where I enjoyed filling fat, five-cent tablets with a hodgepodge of drawings," he said. "I drew for hours at a time just for the fun of it. Yet I was hoping to find some practical reason to draw for the rest of my life."

He loved to doodle on a pad he kept in his desk at school. He also drew on the margins of the pages in his textbooks. Sometimes Peet's drawing got him in trouble. Most of the time his teachers would catch him and scold him. But one teacher was different.

"This particular teacher snatched my tablet away just as the others had done and marched to the front of the room with it," Peet said. "Then turning to the class she said, 'I want you to see what William has been doing!' Then with an amused smile, the teacher turned the pages for all to see. After returning the tablet she encouraged me with, 'I hope you will do something with your drawing someday.'"

The teacher's words made Peet feel better. He also felt good during the school's used book sale. "My illustrated books were best sellers," he said.

LEARNING FROM NATURE & ADVENTURE

Peet loved to explore nature. He and his friends went on pretend safaris. Once Peet sent for information about a real safari. Then he learned he could not afford it.

Peet also worked on his grandfather's farm in southern Indiana. Peet could play with lots of animals. He enjoyed learning about each animal's unique personality.

"Animal personalities have always intrigued me," he said. "The desire to find out more about them made a reader out of me. Our neighborhood library was an old frame mansion crammed full of books. Even though it was about four miles away, I was a regular customer in the worst winter weather."

Trains also fascinated young Peet. He would sneak down to the railway station to watch the trains come and go. Then he would sketch them. He also sold newspapers at the famous Indianapolis 500 Speedway. Peet loved the extra money, and the chance to draw something different.

"For a few days after the race I drew dozens of race cars in action," he said. "Some of the crackups I'd seen. Wheels flying off, cars hurtling over the wall, and some exploding into flames. Yet I was never a racing fan and never cared who won the 500."

Peet did care about football. It was one of his favorite games, despite his small size. "At age eleven I was serious about becoming a football star," he said. " I would have gladly traded my drawing ability for a few pounds of muscle."

Twenty-three cars spurting into action at the start of the 500-mile Memorial Day auto race in Indianapolis, Indiana, 1934.

Football became even more of a dream after Peet left grade school. His grandmother had died, so his family had to move. Now he had to attend Tech High School—one of the country's biggest high schools.

ALMOST A FAILURE

Peet's first year at Tech High School was a disaster. "Life had become much too serious to be dreaming about an art career," he said. "So I didn't enroll in any art classes." Instead, Peet took classes like algebra, English and Latin. He failed every one except physical education. He had to do something different.

A friend suggested he take art courses. Peet gave it a try. For the next four years, his art classes inspired him to study other subjects.

Eventually, he received a scholarship from the John Herron Art Institute in Indianapolis. It was a dream come true.

"My dream of making art a career suddenly seemed much more realistic," he said. He also loved the school. "It was all peaches and cream. No devilish academic problems to boggle my mind."

People noticed Peet's work. The 1933 Tech High School yearbook included one of his drawings. One of his paintings won a red ribbon at the 1934 Indiana State Fair Art Exhibition. Another painting won a prize, and appeared in the Sunday paper.

In art school, Peet noticed Margaret Brunst, the woman who sat next to him. It took a long time before he talked to her. Then they got to know each other well. They planned to get married when Peet found a job that paid enough to support them.

Finding such a job was hard. The country had just endured the Depression. Many people did not have jobs. For a while, Peet drew department store ads. He also worked for a greeting card company. But his career did not take off until he went to Los Angeles, California.

AN IN-BETWEENER

A friend suggested that Peet apply for a job at Walt Disney Studios. The friend had heard they were looking for artists. "It was no time to be choosy," said Peet. "So I filled out the application, dashed off the required sketches, and stuck them in the mail." When Peet returned home after losing his greeting card job, a letter was waiting for him. Walt Disney Studios invited him to a job tryout.

An overhead view of Pershing Square in Los Angeles, California,
about the time Bill Peet arrived.

Peet hitched a ride to Los Angeles and found a place to live. On the first day of the tryout, he drew pictures of Mickey Mouse, Donald Duck and Goofy. The studio was looking for artists whose style was similar to Walt Disney's. By the end of the month, Peet was one of three artists who had passed the test.

Disney Studios hired Peet as an "in-betweener" for $22.50 a week. He added drawings in between other drawings to make the characters move. Peet found the work boring. But it paid the bills. It also gave him a shot at other Disney projects like *Snow White and the Seven Dwarfs*. It was Disney's first feature-length animated film. Peet drew some scenes.

Peet wrote to Margaret as soon as he got the job. She joined him in Los Angeles. They were married November 30, 1937.

Peet knew he had to do something special at work. Otherwise, he might be an in-betweener forever. His chance came when the studio announced plans for a new movie called *Pinocchio*. The studio needed zany characters to inhabit a place called Bogyland.

Peet sent sketches and waited a long time. Meanwhile, he kept drawing.

NO MORE DUCKS!

One day, Peet couldn't take it anymore. He had been drawing scene after scene of Donald Duck. "After drawing him a few thousand times, I had begun to despise him," he said about Donald Duck. "It was too much! I went berserk and shouted at the top of my voice, 'NO MORE DUCKS!' much to the horror of my fellow in-betweeners."

The next day, Peet almost didn't return to his office. He was certain his boss would fire him because of his outburst. Yet when he returned to pick up his jacket, he found a letter. It said the people creating *Pinocchio* liked his zany characters, and wanted him to work for them.

Peet went to work on *Pinocchio*. He also met Walt Disney. Soon, he found working with Disney was not easy. When he saw the finished version of *Pinocchio*, Peet realized his name was nowhere in the credits.

"Walt was very sensitive about credit," Peet said. "He would say, 'We are all in this together'. But what he meant was, the credit is all mine. I knew that WE stood for Walter Elias. Everything came out 'Walt Disney presents.' The rest of our names might as well have been in the phone book."

Peet's next project was *Fantasia*. After that, he worked on *Dumbo*. Peet developed a large part of the *Dumbo* story himself. He enjoyed that. Margaret had given birth to their son, Bill Jr., about the same time. Peet patterned parts of the baby elephant after his own baby son.

Peter Pan came next. So did World War II. The studio's workload changed overnight. They made films for the war effort. Some films were made to teach people. Others encouraged them to buy bonds to finance the war. Still others made the United States' enemies look very bad.

When the war ended, Peet worked on *Song of the South*. He planned the tales of Br'er Rabbit, Br'er Fox and Br'er Bear. Finally, Peet was more than a sketch artist.

Illustrator Bill Peet surrounded by a collection of drawings for
the animated Disney film *The Sword and the Stone*.

SEEKING A VOICE
OF HIS OWN

Cinderella was Disney's next project. Peet drew
mice and cat characters. In the evenings, he
worked on a second career, drawing cartoons.
He sent some cartoons to magazines, but they
came back rejected.

This is part of the vast facilities of the Walt Disney studio in Burbank, California, 1942.

Peet tried his hand at another longtime dream—storybooks. He often made up stories for his sons, Bill and Steve. Now, he put those stories and characters on paper. It was easy to draw the figures. The storywriting was hard.

"I could visualize the characters and also picture the stories from beginning to end," he said. "But when it came to writing them I was at a loss for words." Peet struggled to write better. Working for Disney made writing even harder. His job came first. Peet worked on *Peter Pan*, *Alice in Wonderland,* and *Sleeping Beauty*.

At the same time, Peet told Walt Disney about a story book he'd written called *Goliath II*. It was about a five-inch-tall elephant. Disney said Peet should turn it into an animated film. For some reason, Peet found that easier than working on his own books.

Famed American cartoonist and movie animator, Walt Disney.

"It finally occurred to me that as long as it was Walt Disney's [story], I could write it," he said. "But when it came to doing a book for myself, I could never complete one."

That pattern changed in 1959. Peet sold his storybook *Hubert's Hair-Raising Adventure* to a publisher. The book is about a lion that has problems growing a new mane.

Peet was thrilled to see his very own book in the bookstores. Yet he wasn't ready to work for himself. He did more Disney films based on his storybooks. Then he got a special phone call from Walt Disney. Disney wanted Peet to plan a movie based on a book titled *One Hundred and One Dalmatians*. Peet said he would do it all— write a screenplay, do the storyboards, and record voices for the characters. It was his biggest job ever.

Dalmatians was so successful Disney gave Peet another job. He wrote a screenplay based on the book *The Sword in the Stone*. The book is about King Arthur as a young man. Next, Peet convinced Disney to base a film on Rudyard Kipling's *Jungle Book*.

GOOD-BYE, WALT DISNEY

By Peet's 49th birthday, five of his books were in print. That day, he and Walt Disney had a fight. Peet decided it was time to go out on his own. After 27 years with Disney, he quit. He told Margaret it was a birthday present to himself.

The next day, Peet began illustrating *Randy's Dandy Lions*. It's a story about five circus lions who are too shy to do their tricks. Next, he wrote *Chester the Worldy Pig*. More than any other book, *Chester* includes parts of Peet's own life. It's about a pig that grows up in Indiana. No one recognizes Chester's talent for balancing his snout on a fence post. So Chester heads West to join the circus, where he becomes a star.

"When Chester becomes the center of attention in the big tent show, that could be the recognition I have received for my books," Peet said. "Which have been printed in many languages and read by kids all over the world."

Peet followed *Chester* with many more books. Some featured friendly animal characters such as Pamela Camel, Buford the Little Bighorn and Merle the High-Flying Squirrel. Finally, Peet was living his dream.

"My early ambition to illustrate animal stories was finally realized," he said. "And a little bit more, since I had never considered writing one. This way I can write about things I like to draw, which makes it more fun than work. And I still carry a tablet around with me and sneak a drawing into it now and then."

"Sometimes I feel like I'm basically doing the same thing as when I was six years old," he added. "Drawing lions and tigers in books."

WE LOVE YOU, BILL!

Peet's work has captured many awards. The *New York Times Book Review* said, "Children in four states have chosen Peet as their favorite author in annual state polls."

Peet's success comes from his detailed drawings. And his characters are often warm and friendly. They invite readers to share in their problems. They also try to overcome their problems with creativity and resourcefulness.

In 1967, judges named Peet outstanding Hoosier author of children's literature. In 1976, his book *How Droofus the Dragon Lost His Head* won the Colorado Children's Book Award and the California Reading Association Young Reader Medal. Peet also won a prestigious Caldecott honor for his autobiography, *Bill Peet: An Autobiography*, which he published in 1989.

Despite all the awards, Peet is most satisfied by entertaining and delighting children with his stories. "My favorite compliment from the kids is, 'We think your books are funny and make us laugh,'" he said. "If you are trying to get kids to read, a book should be entertaining. If it isn't fun, it becomes a chore."

Bill Peet, American author and illustrator.

GLOSSARY

Animated film — motion picture made up of drawings.

Bonds — a certificate issued by a government which promises to pay back with interest the money borrowed from the buyer of the certificate.

Depression — a time in the history of the United States when most people had very little money.

Doodle — to draw or make marks in an absent-minded way while talking or thinking.

Drafted — when a person has to serve in the military.

Hoosier — nickname for a person from the state of Indiana.

Illustrate — to draw.

Manipulate — to operate something with your hands.

Storyboards — illustrated boards that show what will be happening in an animated film.

INDEX